Stage to Page

Poems from the Theater

Also by James B. Nicola

Manhattan Plaza
(poetry)

Playing the Audience:
The Practical Actor's Guide to Live Performance
(non-fiction)

Stage to Page

Poems from the Theater

by James B. Nicola

Word Poetry

Published by Word Poetry
P.O. Box 541106
Cincinnati, OH 45254-1106

ISBN: 978-1-62549-187-9

Poetry Editor: Kevin Walzer
Business Editor: Lori Jareo

Visit us on the web at www.wordpoetrybooks.com

Cover art: "Diver Near Saturn's Moon," 2003. Polaroid
Sonnegram by Eve Sonneman. Courtesy of Nohra Haime
Gallery, New York, and Eve Sonneman, New York

Acknowledgments

Thanks to my readers: James Cleveland, Anne Delano, Mary Guzzy, Richard Maurer, Juliana Meehan, and Alan Tongret, whose feedback was so helpful. Thanks also to cover artist Eve Sonneman. And buckets of gratitude to those who pored through these poems pre-publication to provide comments for the back cover, whose names are blazoned thereon.

* * *

Grateful acknowledgment is made to the editors of the following publications and web-sites where poems first appeared:

"1985," in *Ladowich* and *Manhattan Plaza*; "Almost Like," in *Cortland Review*; "And Charlie Chaplin is no more," in *Spindrift*; "Antigone," in *Mobius*; "Billing," in *Aries*; "Clown," in *Existere*; "Denizen," "The Hungry," "Life of the Party," "Lincoln Center," "Touring," and "The Waiters," in *Manhattan Plaza*; "Diction," in *Now Culture*; "Elocutionary Advice" and "The Wit," in *Parody*; "Fermata," in *Poetry Salzburg*; "Hellsgate," in *Fickle Muses*; "In The Dimness," in *NY _____ (NY Underscore)* and *Manhattan Plaza*; "Misanthrope," in *Trinacria*; "Miss Lee," in *Loch Raven Review*; "On Staging with No Bows," in *Word Gumbo*; "Outdoor Drama," in *The Neovictorian/Cochlea*; "Play," in *Blue Unicorn*; "Shakespeare," in *Alimentum*; "Shakespearean Actor," in *Serving House Journal*; "Sylvius," in *Upstart Crow*; "Time," in *Listening Eye*; "Tip from the Taxi Driver," in *Dos Passos Review*; "Touring Artist," in *Iron Horse Literary Review*; "Yesterday's Man," in *Third Wednesday*.

Dedication

To

those

who

have

taken

the

plunge

or

are

about

to

.

.

.

Preface

The poems in the present volume have been inspired not only by the live drama, but also by the realms of song, dance, and cinema.

And to borrow a phrase from film credits, please be aware that no actual person, living or dead, should be construed as represented in these poems—except where mentioned expressly by name, of course. The verse has been hewn out of welters of experience fertilized by imagination—and vice versa.

Welcome to my world.

—JBN

The symbol

$$\Delta$$

at the bottom of a page indicates a blank line between sections of a poem wherever that line is lost in pagination.

A title *in italics* indicates an untitled poem identified by its first line or phrase.

* * *

Several of these poems feature epigraphs or postscripts, but should you want an explanation (or reminder) of other references literary or dramatic, supplemental notes appear on pages 105-108 for your convenience.

Table of Contents

Act Three

To Players

You are not what you are, but what you're not;
you're what you can be, and the opposite.
That is, after all, what makes art, art.
When a master, you're a servant; when
a lackey, be a guide. All you have mem-
orized must seem spontaneous, to them,
as it was yesterday, will be again
tomorrow; what you over-pronounce, seem
uttered, merely. Your love affairs will end
at curtain, resume from where you began,
not from where you left off: they don't pretend
to develop like life. And on like this
till closing night. And though together you're
to make a mirror, your images shall
be moving, sharp—re*lived*, not just reported.
Your glass stands a little bit distorted,
though—a smoky, well-smudged, fun house mirror—
so that it's up to them whether they see
themselves in it or not, laugh, cry, rise, fall
with the action, see themselves suddenly clearer,
or blink and never see themselves at all.
But for two hours, two and a half, three,
you tease, toast, remind guests not how it is,
merely, but how it has been, and could be:
make them feel fortunate the tragedy
is not what is, and have them understand
it need not ever be; in comedy,
you let them play their roles with dignity
in the orchestra, mezzanine, or balcony,
safe from pratfalls, hijinks, or being made
to look like a fool. After all, that's your

job, your charge, your calling, your stock-in-trade—
that, and making them think they're having fun
so that they can't help but come back for more.
So welcome. Now. Act One. Scene One. Page one.

Act One

The Beauty of Actors

Their silences are sinew and connect
the muscle of their actions with the tis-
sue of their words so that you keep expect-
ing their next rash deed. Whatever it is,
you're unable *not* to find out! The wis-
dom in their looks holds back their sounds with dis-
cipline, its fire invisible, like a
volcano not erupting. I once saw
an active one a week before it blew.
How it reminded me of, what, the beau-
ty of actors, as they've made me stop, think,
suspect a trace of smoke, breathe in, and blink
    as a Cypriot watching, from an aproned shore,
    the goddess emerge from the sea foam, wanting more.

Audition Tips

Speak boldly: Thrill—as if your life depend-
ed on it (which it does if you're a pro)!

The inmost will, the hidden hope—extend,
that caring drench the hall.
                              Let casters know
you intimately, and a world beyond,
and then decide.
                         Let stillness need to move,
then not, as if a secret kept you still;
treat Silence as possession from above,
thought focused forward, as a rankled will.

Let strangers be like lovers, who respond
without words, remembering there's no such thing
as Monologue.
                    Let each response surprise
you, the ten-thousandth time or first.
                                              And sing
so warmed, so stoked, that sparks shoot from your eyes,
fed from a furnaced soul, the actor's wand.

Elocutionary Advice

You might engage your jowls
To gather round your vowels.
And consonants slide better
With lips a little wetter.

Billing

We are not what we are but who you say
we are. That is the business of the show,
which makes us what we are each time we speak
onstage, all memorized and set to play
six evening and two matinées a week.
And if an evening's pangs of thought and laughter
enthrall you to your feet to shout *Bravo,*
then for the next show, or the one right after,

our agents can negotiate for billing
above the title (wouldn't that be thrilling?)
or boxed and on a separate line, below,
that you might notice and begin to know
the name associated with the star,
as well as what we, who we, that we are.

Clown

I don't imagine meeting kings and queens.
But we were born not to rise and arrive,
but rise and fall again and again fall,
half-needing black and blue marks to survive!
No clown believes in learning to behave:

So, though there may be royals we appall,
our job's to entertain, cheer up, and stave
off your dark looks and thoughts by our bright miens,
and not bow to the few, nor most, but all—
and, one or two, in a bad way, maybe, save.

The Supernumerary

Twelve men of muscle—left. On cue, each in turn scoops
a dangerous-appearing, albeit harmless, spear.
They strut out on the stage as just as many troops.
(I watched once from the wings. How their swagger stirred
    fear
in my heart with a start from the sparks in their eyes!)
But each knows his job and keeps focused on the star
speaking center, and draws your focus there likewise
so you never worry, or wonder who they are.

What, then, pulls your focus away from center stage?
The third from the right, facing outward, makes a crack
in the wall, smoldering impatiently with rage—
but in two seconds turns professionally back.

Once more the weekly paycheck is a mighty thing
to keep a soldier waiting in a line, or wing.

Shakespearean Actor

He started in the mail room, barely speak-
ing English. But he was never too shy
to ask what a word signified, or phrase,

and say it, over and over. Every week
he learned a sonnet, then two, then the plays,
one paperback per pocket. How he'd try

to contain himself, and stuff the slots—until
a temporary fellow worker caught
him reading, one who just happened to be

a sometime actor—who, one off-day, brought
the immigrant along to a "look-see,"
which is a tryout where they only look.

But they asked him to read a bit, impressed
that he had brought with him a giant book
with the title The Compleat Works of Wil-

liam Shakespeare. I should think he passed the test,
for he's been happy onstage now for years,
conveying sundry messages, and spears.

Educational Drama

Their motives for trying out, varied as
the number in the hall, were never known.
Not to themselves, not to each other.

But in the end, it was the humpy physics
major who got cast, not as Paris
(a perfect role for some fit novice), nor
as one of the scene-one rowdies who bite
thumbs and jeer (all roles optimally served
by well-groomed thighs as well)—but Romeo;

and Juliet was an acne'd shy thing
who'd signed up for the class just for the credit;

while it was the serious actors who
played Tybalt (who dies early), Benvolio
(who's required to listen to Romeo for several acts),
Paris, and Lady Capulet. The Nurse
and Friar were four-eyed freshmen, surely virgins,
from outside the department, chemistry
and anthropology. Lord Capulet,
self-styled dweeb, could barely speak! The stars
of the department, many, had to dance
at the masked ball, dressed down by the swishy Prince
(cast sibilant, for the director was
a feminist—and Lesbian, some said).
And some of them were barely seen again,
save for the crowd scenes. Unbelievable.

Well, the production seemed so out of whack
that the chairman of the drama department dis-

invited the respondent from the Kennedy Center
and uncast majors sneered; those cast, knew better.

But by week two you couldn't get a ticket.
The science majors filled one house, then told
their friends who told their friends who told *their* friends.
An article got published, how the play
was life itself. The President even came
and wept, it was reported. Who cares? More
important is what's happened to the cast
in the decades since that destined travesty.

The Friar married the Nurse. They've seven kids
and work together in a research lab
testing new cures. The stutterer Capulet's
a senator. Tybalt volunteers vacations
for Doctors Without Borders. Of the gangs,
two—Balthasar and Samson—work for Greenpeace;
Mercutio, Benvolio, and Gregory
for Legal Aid; while Paris and the Prince
have moved to Massachusetts where they've married.

Juliet and Romeo have not
appeared on stage since then but live in town.
Tuesday nights they answer phones for a hotline
from 8-12, the calls continuous
so neither has the chance to say much else.
But I helped out one Tuesday before Christmas,
a dark time, and I think I saw them blush
when their eyes met between synchronized calls.
She is a beauty now. And he is kind.
Their voices have grown useful saving lives.

And Rosaline, who had no lines to speak
in *Romeo and Juliet,* appears
in movies. You would recognize her name.

Almost Like

The almost actors almost acted out
their almost acted almost acting scene.
The other almost actors in the room
applauded, almost. It was almost like
real acting (almost). Then the almost scene
was shot and spliced into an almost film,
an almost movie almost like a movie
from the time when they made movies like real movies.
The almost audience almost acted like
they almost even enjoyed the almost film.
The almost critics almost praised it, and
the masses found enough to understand,
in the age when painters almost paint, and
writers almost write, readers almost
read, and the almost entire generation
feels almost like we are almost alive.

The Scrupulous

The acting teacher taught a youth
(among the many others there)
with deep-set eyes and raven hair
who suddenly started to emerge
into herhimself, "blossom," quite
remarkably, deliciously—
excruciatingly, in truth.
Heshe had never felt an urge
before so sharp and powerful
that when the student asked himher
to dinner (with a showerful
of gratitude) what could heshe
do, although very grateful for
the invitation, but demur?
It shouldn't be, couldn't be, wouldn't be right.
(Shehe won't be there anymore,
not after this semester's through.
O God, if only I were 22...)

At times heshe stares in a glass
reflecting on that banner class
and all that never happened. Dur-
ing office hours shehe stops by
with an innocent *Thank you, Sir-*
Ma'am for the coaching and the chance
to play a lead. —You're having fun,
then? (How could shehe know better?)
heshe says, glad shehe dropped by
who, next year, will be a senior
and ask himher if heshe would
write a recommendation letter.

(Heshe had said that shehe should
plan applications in advance
for graduate study or a job
insisting it will be *No prob-
lem, not in the least, consider it done!)*
Shehe is still not even 21.

A Round of Applause

An impressionable soul, during her ju-
nior year of high school, tried out for the mu-
sical. A senior told her "you're a shoe-
in for the lead, you're such an ingénue,"

then boffed her. Well, she found enough to do
in the chorus, even had a line or two.
She loved applause, and opted to pursue
the theater, although no one told her to.

The others in the cast were so enthu-
siastic, what they said *had* to be true:
she was not only talented, but beau-
tiful. And now she's living in New York.

Of course she doesn't hear the unkind talk
behind closed doors, auditions. *She is awk-
ward . . . . — Chubby.* But her teachers, whom she pays,
tell her she'll be a star, one of these days.
And payment tempers what a person says.

To meet her, you'd think *What a lovely soul*
and tell her she is sure to land a role.

Life of the Party

The day lily beams orange, from the road,
for one day, then folds up again. Inside
its brief blossom you'll find another shade
of almost-orange, ready to explode.

A tenor upstairs in my building croons
all day, almost unheard, a bona fide
talent. If he went out, he'd have it made.
He tunes a little louder on full moons.

One day I asked him to a party. He
drank, mingled, joked, laughed, put a lamp shade on,
sang thrillingly, and was the last one gone.
For the rest of the year, when he'd see me

in the lobby, he'd turn the other way,
a day lily, lying low, until its day.

The Hungry

The day I brought home Jacob Riis
my father did not look,
uninterested in that kind of book.

And mother said to ride in front
when I had to take the bus,
that the riders in the back were dangerous.

And when the riots were reported in
the news and on TV,
they said I should feel fortunate that we

were not like that. Which made me think
about What if we were,
and I opened the Riis and showed them a picture.

Ma clucked her tongue and rolled her eyes.
Dad issued a directive:
I hate it when he gets over-protective

so I went and joined a theater troupe.
Now I hardly ever speak
to my family. Five days a week

we tour the worse-off boroughs. The
performances we give,
with workshops, bring in just enough to live.

Sometimes we go to prisons or
reformatories—"schools."
It's said to "rehabilitate"—which fools

Δ

only the administrators, if
you want to know the truth.
Yesterday there was a Spofford youth

who wanted to go with us, then
and there, and join our band.
He clenched my wrist. I said I understand

your hunger to escape this place
and join a family,
but didn't like the way he clung to me,

to tell the truth. Ed saw, and asked
to take our photograph,
and said a joke to make the poor kid laugh.

His pals said it was the first time
they'd seen him smile that way.
I said, you don't say. And to this day

I've kept our photo in a book
like Jacob Riis's *How*
the Other Half Lives. It's at my parents' now.

(Jacob Riis was the author—and photographer—of *How the Other Half Lives: Studies Among the Tenements of New York,* published in 1890. It introduced New York's book buying public to the specifics of squalor. Spofford Juvenile Center, renamed Bridges, is in the Bronx)

Touring Artist

He barks of Fellowman's gashes
    and plucks a scathing song.
His charm, guitar, and batted lashes
    gather in a throng.

He champions as he bewails
    the poor man's rusted dreams.
While counting up his CD sales
    he even feels, it seems.

One of his tunes made me laugh
    last year at our county fair.
I went back for an autograph.
    He didn't see me there.

I perched and listened patiently
    while he fingered a new tune
and scratched out lyrics. I thought he
    would have to be finished soon.

Once more from the top, and then—a sigh
    for the family on relief.
I felt a drop in my left eye;
    he soaked his handkerchief.

And I'm still fed by how he feels.
    He signed two CDs I bought.
I've sold them for a month of meals.
    A pretty good deal, I thought.

A Broadway Show

The longest-running Broadway shows, like *Phan-
tom of the Opera* and *Lion King,*
are musicals where audiences can,
if they have heard the score already, sing
along—not out loud, necessarily,
but swaying, smiling. . . . Even subtler than
this sort of audience participation
is that each crowd is automatically
brand new; from such dynamic variation
a certain sort of spontaneity
ensues. And keeping old things fresh is key
to musicals'—or plays'—longevity.
A show can run ten, twenty years or more:
It's not the way that Broadway was before.

A Broadway show that runs a long time will
endure changes of cast. The script, however,
should stay the same. (But when a star gets bill-
ing bigger than the playwright's, she can say
whatever she wants. Poor Tennessee
Williams was lucky to have Laurette Tay-
lor as Amanda in *Menagerie:*
She said the same words—hers—day after day,
but never did deliver, quite, his play.
Because of hers, though, his might last forever—
which is the only version that can be
performed today. The improvised is gone;
the true text, which the playwright penned, lives on.)

And when a Broadway show goes on the road,
the scripted dialogue's supposed to stay
the same, too: though, to save expense or load-

in time, a tour will sometimes simplify
the set. If you want bells and whistles, try
to see a Broadway show, then, on Broadway.

With classic scripts, in the public domain,
an absent author doesn't hold much sway
but, generally, is dead. Producers reign
while diligent directors chop away
whole scenes; remaining dialogue's redacted
so as to be more easily enacted—
or more successfully. The goal's a *hit,*
not faithfulness to an original.

To purists, such adjustment is a sin,
I guess, but what can they do about it?
The *hit*'s the thing, right? (One consolation
to classic authors, though, is that often
the deviation's deep enough to call
the recreated thing an adaptation,
not a revival.)

               At the Times Square Church,
located in a Broadway house of yore,
the variation and improvisation,
to tell the truth, are unbelievable.
(I read the Script back when I was in search
of something good to read—no, something more . . . .)
But what an unbelievable ovation!

How might the Author feel, though (it is said
He lived among us, and is still not dead),
about the trade of purity for pop-
ularity? I wonder—hard. . . . But then
the swing band starts responding with *Amen!*
and sways in unison, the *Hallelu-*
jahs heave, the saxes swell, the brasses bop,

and I rise up to sing in rapture, too—
plus, swear I'll come back next week, and the next,
in spite of alterations to the Text.

It's Broadway, after all! A Broadway show
can run forever now, especially
if it's a musical, as you now know.
Besides, the ticket price is by donation,
which is about the same as being free:
This compensates for all the variation
from the original—at least, to me.

Time

He chews the scenery and forgets his lines,
interpolating inappropriate text
so we cannot be sure what's coming next.
The manager's a coward and never fines
him, though. Worse than a ham, he is a hack,
and yet he must have something that I lack,
the way that he can draw a crowd—in these
road towns, especially. That's why he gets
top billing when he wants it—New Year's Eves,
for instance, when it seems the whole world lets
him lead us in his theme song, Auld Lang Syne.
It's everybody's favorite anthem—mine,
too, since he's got connections in high places.
So sing along and stay in his good graces.

Touring

. . .

They're in the park, Honey. Sorry.

They'll be fine.

Are you kiddin'? Eddie's almost as tall as I am now.
    Besides it's Sunday afternoon, who's going to
    bother—?

Well they waited all morning, what was I supposed to tell
    'em?

That's OK, Honey, I know how those closing night parties
    are.

Because I made them spend yesterday cleaning their
    rooms. I couldn't keep 'em inside the whole weekend.

Ohyeah, gettin' the place ship-shape for you. So when's
    your flight home?

Going where?

Oh.

Are you kiddin'? That's great. "Pilot season" they call it,
    right?

Ohyeah, I know a thing or two about the Business. That
    new agent's working out for us, isn't he? Tour closes
    one day and you get an LA audition the next.

Tuesday, whenever it is. ♫ *Cal-if-or-nia-here-we-come.* ♫

I know, if it's meant to be. But just wait till they see what
    you do with a song.

So when *do* we see you?

Oh.

Oh.

Oh. You kiddin'? That's terrific.

Of course we'll manage. Take as many weeks as you—

'Course they'll be fine, but—

They'll just be sorry they missed you, that's all.

I mean, missed your call.

Why don't you call again tonight?

Well, 9's a little late for Millie.

Remember to change your watch when you get to LA.

9 then. New York time. Millie can go to bed late, this one
time, so she can talk to her mother.

Are you kiddin', Honey? I'm *proud* of you!

I kept tellin' ya, all you needed was the right agent.

Yeah, "Tony," I remember his name.

Uh-huh.

Uh-huh.

Ohyeah. Well, we're going to have to have him to dinner,
then.

He doesn't?

Well the guy's gotta eat some time, doesn't he?

I guess that's why he's so successful I guess.

♫ *California here we—* ♫

Oh, but you will, honey. You will.

I'm not going to jinx you, honey, I'm going to be your *good*
luck charm.

Oh, yes you will, just wait till we show 'em what you do
with a song.

. . .

                              * * *

. . . All, right, Honey, we'll pack up a box for you. You want
to make out a list for us—?

You won't have time to what?

What, you mean *now*?

All right. Oh, no, wait a sec, the pad's here but the pencil's
gone.

—Eddie? Where's the pencil, the one that goes on this
string?

27

Eddie?!

—Wait a sec, Honey.
No, he's not mad, he's just, at that age, he's always loud
    with doors. Wait a sec.

—*Charley? Charley, it's your mother.*
On the phone!
We need to make out a list of things to send her for winter.
Christmas? No, she's not, she just got another tour, big role.

—Just a sec, Honey, I'm looking for the pencil.

—*Charley. Charley, I'm talking to you, don't walk away!*
    Isn't there a pen or pencil anywhere in this
    apartment?
Where did they all go?
OK, Charley, you want to come and talk to her while I look
    for one?

—Honey, hang on, I'll find one somewhere.
No, that's not Millie, that's just the TV.
She's, um, she's having an overnight at—
Ohyeah, a "slumber party." Ha-ha.
Wait a sec, Hon.

—*Millie, shh, don't cry.*
Millie, now come on. Your mother can hear you.
Christmas? No, but we're all going to go join her for
    February vacation, for the whole week.
Yes I promise! Wherever she is.
I don't know, we haven't gotten the itinerary yet, she just
    got the job.
That's the list of places you go on a trip, or on a tour.
    Itinerary.

All right, say "list" then, I'll know what you mean.
I know we promised Christmas, sweetie, but this is your
mother's Big Break. She's playing a lead. And at the
end, in six months, it might end up on Broadway. You
want to see her on Broadway, Millie, don't you?
'Cause we'll have her home then!
OK, Sweetie, I understand but listen, do you know where all
the pencils and pens went?
Oh, my goodness. Wow. A collection. You want to come talk
to your mother?
Oh, darling. No, I'm not mad. That's all right. Come here.
I'll get you all the pencils and pens you want, don't
you worry about it, darling. Shh. Shh. There now.

—Honey, sorry, here I am.
Ohyeah I found a pen.
No, they were all in Millie's desk, in a drawer. You know at
that age, how they, well, she started a collection.
Yeah, all of them.
Well, she misses you, you know.
No, Charley's not here either.
I know it's Sunday morning, but, well, they were counting
on Christmas together this year.
Me? You kiddin', Honey? For that money? And the
opportunity—just wait till everyone sees what you do
with a song!
Honey.
Honey.
Honey, no, I'm your biggest fan, don't forget that.
OK, honey, yes I have the pad. Shoot. I'll make the list.
Yes I can mail it tomorrow. Parcel Post or UPS?
Yup, it's you and me. I'm just ears.
Yes I have a pen, I told you.
Well let me try.

Ohyeah, it writes. Wow, bright purple. Shoot.
. . .

* * *

. . . He's coming at 8:30. You answer the door, all right,
    Eddie?
Because I'm going down to the park. Can't you do this one
    thing for me?
For your mother then?
Good man. Everything's in the boxes—in the bedroom—
Yes he can come in, but tell him to be quiet, so your brother
    and sister don't hear.
If you want to help, that's your business, no skin off my—
On second thought, no, let Tony lug the damn boxes
    himself. Tell him to use the back elevator so he can do
    it all in one trip.
Well she's in rehearsals up to her ears, so she can't come.
I'm sure she would.
That would be nice, surprise her opening night. You're a
    good man.
Ohyeah of course you're old enough to take Charlie and
    Millie to the theater without me.
Well all right if you don't want to, you don't have to, but
    she'll be in the neighborhood six days a week, she'd
    love to see more of all three of you.
Because she'll have time between the matinées and
    evenings, every Wednesday and Saturday.
Are you kiddin'? Because she's your mother. You should be
    proud of her.
No, don't say that.
No she loves you.
Don't say that.
Eddie, Eddie, no. You don't understand.
Wait till you see what she does with a song. . . .

Fermata

She held the high note, or held what she had,
as a gift the dark sea of gentility
could not refuse. . . .

                  The gowns rocked with the wave,
ballasted to their velvet seats. Had you
been deaf, you might as easily have suspected
a sudden epidemic of hemorrhoids.
The tuxes riffled as some sleeves rotated
that eyes might steal glances at watches, masked
by cuffs of sleeves; other arms rose like a
baton striking an inconspicuous upbeat
(their watches closer to the heart, but harder
to get to, on fobs in stylish waistcoat pockets)
then completed the cycle in a downbeat of
unvoiced, attentive, polite desperation.
The ensemble of the audience, then, was still
as mice in a tempest, reluctant to
scurry, so as not to enrage the storm.

Her accompanist nodded, signaling release,
but she did not let go. (Iván remarked
he'd never seen a soprano smile so well
on "O" before. *Or for so long,* said Carlotta.)

Later in private she explained the true
liberation implied at each fermata,
the trust required. He kept playing for her.

                                             Δ

She wore light satin gowns with gloves and pearls—
even rehearsing her cadenzas and portamenti—
but was invited to perform only
that once. She's planning to tour Europe soon.

The Waiters

If you were to meet
your expert waiter on the street
and chat with him or her,
you would discover
that she or he is actually more:
an undiscovered singer, actor,
dancer, musician, artist, or author.

In New York
waiting is the work
whereby we pay our rent,
but not what we are meant
to do forever, as a career.

Were you to inquire
how long I have waited,
you'd see how dedicated
to my art I am, and call
me a professional.
The road to stardom's rarely straight,
you know. So I wait.
No, not to be a waiter,
but for later.

Act Two

To Playwrights

What the journalist hammers to expose,
you fashion as a feather to invoke
wonder by tickling just outside the nose,
under the chin. The power of a joke

is one of your disciplines, too. Outrage
and shock, sure, but when the mirror's clearly
an unabridged reflection of the age,
beware the "truth" too raw or too sincerely

expressed; a spectator who understands
for the first time, if sitting on their hands,
is no good. Rather, orchestrate the facts
so as to get your audience to relax,

accept, breathe, listen, keep their minds and hearts
open to the events of your evening.
That's why you dedicate supporting parts
to comic relief, or have the tenor sing—

to entertain, not lull, but hold them there
glued gladly in the stalls chair after chair,
believing they are safe, that, later, they
might think about what happened in your play,

then wake up in the middle of a night
as if struck by a strange dawn's sudden light—
which fades fast but returns, as you well know,
the next time theater-goers like you go.

Things

A thing
that's not a thing
is the thing
that is The Thing.

But a thing
that is a thing
is the thing
whereby the thing

that's not a thing—
that is, the thing
that *is* The Thing—
is thung.

The What

The finger of a god about to touch
a newborn reaching. . . . A sneaked kiss averted
and now the object of a love, alerted. . . .

What is there is still there, but isn't much
compared to what's not, once the pump is primed.

In both the plastic and performing arts,
craft is the glue which binds impatient parts,
the grease which keeps them gearing, and the air
which keeps them buoyant that one breath well-timed
flick the feather of an angel so it's seen—
with a gasp such that no honest spirit care
what content, form, mad strokes, or lush words mean,
but see that what is there is what's between,
what's imminent: a birth, a love affair. . .

What For

as in the drama, not for the stage but what is in the air;
as in the design, not for the structure, but for the space;
as in the music, not for the notes, but the shiver up a spine;
as in the dance, not for the steps but for the pause between;

as in the kiss, not for the two, but the breath that makes
    two one;
as in the maths, not for Greek figures, but what's invoked,
    not there;
so in the poetry, not for the words, but the after-beats
    beyond
a solution—wonder,
          more wonder,
                vicarious ecstasy

The wrong place

The wrong place at the wrong time—
    don't two wrongs make a right?
At least, don't double negatives
    like *not not* or *not night*

imply a glimmer in the gloom,
    a slack in Fate's flung rope
that her hungry noose might be slipped from
    by a hummingbird of hope?

Now, *the wrong place at the* right *time,*
    and *the right one at the wrong,*
are eggs that hatch a darker bird
    who'll sing a tragic song—

a raven caught in a beaver trap,
    or starling, crow, or chough
that craves and strays like the man who wants
    and cannot have enough.

But *wrong-wrong* is a circumstance
    of plot complexity
that upside-downs the grimaced mask—
    a cause for comedy.

Moments

A playwright sees, at any moment, eight
to twenty ways each character might act:
lash out at once; plot secretly and wait
developments; exhibit charm and tact,

the flame on simmer so the stew won't burn;
or plant insinuation like a seed
to fertilize and only later learn
what nasty organism it will breed.

Likewise the other characters conceal
the permutations of their smoldering plights
until they are so moved as to reveal
when, in a breath, a spark within *ignites*.

Although the dramatist expects by curtain
the outcome wrought so deftly in the play,
the best performance is when no one's certain
tonight's performance will turn out that way.

Diction

I'm studying old movies, black and white,
to hear the way they talked in parlor drama
and speak as smoothly, or at least to write
speeches without a dangling clause or comma.

Since I still have a pile of DVDs
to get through, you won't see me for a while;
not till I have acquired some expertise
at choosing words with confidence of style

and clarity of purpose. If I can't,
then I'll script something for the silver screen.
They'll have to cast someone like Cary Grant
to get across exactly what I mean.

Then I'll invite you to a private screening,
warn you the story's been inspired, but not
quite based, on real life, if you get my meaning.
They'll also need someone like Randolph Scott . . . .

> (Randolph Scott and Cary Grant were
> movie stars and friends. Good friends)

My friend Harry Koutoukas

My friend Harry Koutoukas said at a symposium
a string of things worth jotting down. He had that way with
 him.
Nostalgia is the death of Art, for one, and, *In the end
we've only Sentiment, after all.* He was that sort of friend.
And that *the fertilizer of Art* (I'd add *of Life* as well)
is Decadence (which ancestors had only lived to tell).
Plus other paradoxes, mingling first with last, and last
with first. Like after Armageddon, when the world is past,
those who are left shall be the last of us, but, too, the first
of who's to come. And who's to say if they'll be blessed or
 cursed?
Of lasts and firsts and bests and worsts and pasts and yets,
 I'm wary.
Certain friends and poets make me think this way. Like
 Harry.

(Harry Koutoukas, Greenwich
Village surrealist playwright)

"The Producers"

To those who were shocked
by *Springtime for Hitler*
in a certain musical comedy

I say, Better him mocked
and derided, made littler,
than passed over cursorily.

And Mel Brooks fought in WW II.
. . . Did you?

Tom Stoppard

Tom Stoppard, b. 1937,
Czech-born British author of many plays including
Rosencrantz and Guildenstern are Dead, *1966,*
which opens with a coin-tossing game;
and The Invention of Love, *1997,*
about A. E. Housman, 1859-1936, English poet,
where Housman is played by two actors, one a youth

The first time I was shaken meeting him
he had set Hamlet's sidekicks on the stage
coin-flipping in Purgatory or Lim-
bo—some between place, of a timeless age,
like death and life at once. Those are the tricks
of theatre which for me was still a hobby.
Their play lit up the darkened panorama
with sparks, struck home, and took my breath away.

Last night the man himself stood in the lobby
of the Lyceum to see his latest drama.
I went and shook his hand. Then, in the play,
I flipped when Housman, punting down the Styx,
went to his younger, sparkling self and took
that other Housman's hand in his—and shook.

Focus

You're staying focused. Someone passing through
rehearsal asks (assuming it's a break
and that they feel important) *How are you?*
To you, you're clearly busy. The mistake
persists and they repeat the question, and
insist you give a moment you *don't have*
to them. You see they'll never understand
the theater, and there's nothing that can save
them from you, so *you* save *them* and seethe: "BUSY—
EXCUSE ME—(Aargh!)" . . . It's kinder to be curt.

To others, theater folk seem crude, or dizzy,
but we stay focused. No one's really hurt.
They're not important: they'll get over it,
you say—if wrong, you pray the show's a hit
and wonder: should you try to change your ways?
For everyone's important, nowadays.

Two Ages

The elder actor squeezed the younger's arm
sharply. The younger started with a yelp.
He sat low in his chair, like half a slob,
oblivious, as teen-age boys are wont.
The elder squeezed again. The youth said, "Don't
do that. Ow!" though the squeeze was not to harm
but to inform the younger, a beginner,
extremely talented and last year's winner
of Best Newcomer. This was his first job
since then. He didn't think he needed help
but finally figured out what was amiss
when he saw the director glaring now
at him. With the third squeeze he sat up, whis-
pering an elongated, grateful *Owwwww*.

Freelance Director

His mania is not tilting, but quixotic
nonetheless—making windmills where there's none
and then making us see them as he sees
them, not as windmills. If a tad psychotic,
his is a calculated frenzy, one
expert in superficialities
as well as depths and the invisible
so that once he's gone, when the house is full,
the music starts to stir, and the lights go dim,
the void fills with itself, ourselves, and him.

Opening

Tonight the haunted house will open. We
should find out soon if all that we have done
is anything, and if we're anyone.

Last night this was a ghost town, only us
inhabiting, exquisitely well-versed
in what we've learned, but for each other only,

and the empty seats beyond. What we've rehearsed
and what we haven't, what's spontaneous,
we share and show tonight. If we survive

beyond tonight, remains for us to see,
for new ghosts to decide when they arrive.
But what we've been is, as of now, too lonely,
so tonight, for a night at least, we come alive.

Complicity

But all the well-timed door slams, funny bits,
deportment, flair, and thought-out, picked-up cues,
plus personal plight with which you infuse
the plot, act only as barbiturates,
save for complicity. Get those who've got
no lines to utter to the very verge
of speaking, feeling, doing. Tacit text
can sizzle; share yours with them as their own.
They'll want to speak and wonder what comes next,
less likely to indulge another urge
like getting up to go, or getting lost
right in their seats, or checking their cell phone.
What's more: you might deflect the rankling thought
of what the tickets and the sitter cost.

The Director

It was a problematic birth, conceived
with angels' succor, nursed through pregnant weeks
of nourishing when no one else believed
in it. It yelled and kicked its limbs when peeved,
when it was coiled within you. Now it speaks

without you, born and well bred. And it does
you proud, a living made thing, with your name—
you drop by only now and then because
you have to let it grow from what it was
to what will break your heart. It is the same

and not the same! And in the dark you know
that all your blood and raw experience
fill only the last seat in the back row
where you are silent now and watch the show
innocuous as any audience.

Civility

should separate an audience from an-
imals as chair arms should contain a rage,
and civilization define the man.
It does—until the crinkling of a page
of a program, or of lozenges unwrapped
during the tenderest of scenes onstage;
or till my hundred dollar seat is slapped
not once but kicked again and again. A cough
can't be kept in, but when alarms go off,
or cell phones—when we've just been civilly
reminded to turn them off—civility
begins to wane. In days of yore, one's gauge
was flinging a glove sharply on the floor.
Of course people don't duel anymore,
but next time, I'll do just that—not to kill,
but frighten, like a madman, maybe give
a long due civics lesson, or a thrill:
they'll watch me blast things from a windowsill,
then thank me, gladly, when I let them live.

Outdoor Drama

The stage set, the chairs glazed with dew of morning,
the quiet of a twenty-hour intermission.
Red birds revel in the rows for crumbs and scraps,
acolytes' unintentional offering
of popcorn grains and cookie remains. They
are loud, inspecting every plastic seat
like cormorants cleansing other souls' detritus
and searching ever for a little better

like last night's audience, intrepid, hopeful,
and dwindling—an inverse proportion to
world numbers. There's an eerie in the empty—
unfelt, though there, in the outside world's fast coil.
Here's peace of a darkened stage, where what has been,
what's yet to come, lies, right before my eyes.

Play

One problem with acting in a hit play
or series, the same role day after day
in perpetuity, is that you may
well "lose"—for want of any better word—
yourself.

        If you're in theater, you've heard
of Eugene O'Neill's father, James the actor,
who toured the *Count of Monte Cristo,* made
his fortune, and became the role he played.
His need to succeed, like Faust's, was a factor
too, of course.

           But then think of George Reeves,
and ask around. Not everyone believes
he shot himself because of being typecast,
his wedding in the offing. Some think he
was murdered, somehow. It's a mystery
even to this day. Nevertheless,
subsequent Supermen have learned to last:
Christopher Reeve and, I believe, Dean Cain—
and actresses who have played Lois Lane.

Then think *Gunsmoke.* Matt Dillon?—James Arness.
Miss Kitty, played by—who?—Amanda Blake.
And Dillon's deputy, comic sidekick,
the hillbilly, what was his name? Festus.
That actor's name? Has it gone up in smoke?

Of course an actor's happy for employ-
ment, and I do feel fortunate the name

my character's been given is the same
as mine. If either one's forgettable,
at least I've found the two compatible,
and one that, for the most part, I enjoy.

On Staging with No Bows

There was no curtain; it was in the round.
Then everything stopped. No one made a sound
and no one bowed, which would have let us know
that it was time to clap, get up, and go.
We couldn't just leave, what with corpses all
over the stage and peppering the hall:
Haemon, at last with his Antigone;
Ismene, there; there, Aunt Eurydice,
who, taking her life, made a widower
of King Creon. Although we knew they were
just actors, and that they would resurrect
themselves, none of the audience expect-
ed them to take so long, or their stillness
to inflict us with a paralysis
that strikes me, even now, writing this.

Antigone

There is another way that we can know
    besides the fits and starts and finishes
        of facts, experience, and trials. There are
the whispers in the womb. Besides the slow
        but steadying bombardments, adolescent's
        cured rages, habits hammered in by parents,
    there are the disappearance of a star
and musings upon why it vanishes

    or reappears, a twinkle in the night
        like tingles in the skin, and inwardly
unfurled perceptions, or the blind man's glow
    when he is sure that something is not right.
        But close your eyes to see and what you see,
no one will persuade you it's not so.

Fate, Four Variations

1.

The diva who goes out once a night to do the torch
song, and gets top billing. The rest of the company
hate her some nights, getting the most applause, but
there's nothing to do about it, that's the contract.

2.

It's not the biggest role but one that never leaves the
stage. From the wings it looks as if she blends into the
scenery, but when she takes stage center her speeches
are the most crucial of the act. Some principals have
come off certain that they saw her mouthing their
dialogue along with them while they spoke, and think
they should put her in a prompter's booth like in
the opera.

3.

I hear the playwright's name's a pseudonym and *she*'s
the author really, incognito, an upstart crow who wants
to be anonymous, a queen with a nasty secret low-
brow habit . . .

4.

I think the role's in every play that's written. But not
appearing since the Middle Ages in the *dramatis
personae*—except as narrators or imps who appear and
disappear mysteriously, or experimental conceits—
modern times she has not per se been cast. Yet.

Yesterday's Man

Yesterday's Man's not gone but in the *sous-*
sol of a long abandoned theater, un-
derneath the stage. Today's Man is the new
production, stressing struts with his cast of one,
forgetting that the floor is laced with traps.
He ad-libs, going up on every line,
deluded that the captive audience claps
and hoots because they think his acting fine.

Tomorrow's lies somewhere in wait for him,
beyond the lights if not behind a curtain—
somewhere that, if he's lit, the lights are dim
enough to make his entrance cue uncertain.

There he is in the wings! You see him too?
He'll signal downstairs right before his cue.

Hellsgate

I once saw a huge head of Hellsgate
in a picture book called Olde Folk Tales.
    The opposite page
    showed the rest of the stage
of a mummers' play touring through Wales.

The face of the head was all twisted
and mottled with sores, warts and moles
    and the biggest damn maw
    you ever saw
hungry for passing souls

from the back of the pub, or the tar pits,
or the next- or the next-to-next town,
    down which you would be sent
    if you didn't repent.
And it looked like a long way down.

* * *

Since then, I've seen myriad movies
full of horror, vice, grossness and gore
    where the portal to hell
    was a myth to dispel
only to visit once more.

One night in the rear of a tavern
patrons quite unabashedly chattered
    about stealing and cheating

on taxes and beating
their wives as if none of it mattered.

Then I saw on the back door a door plaque
with a hells-mouth from which rose a laughter
    so piercing and scar-
     y I raced out of there.
I keep hearing it, though, decades after.

Shakespeare

My KRUPPS® is on the blink, but you should taste
the coffee at my house. I've dusted off
my Grandma's classic four-piece counter-top
drip pot. It's mostly metal. Its black handles
and knob still hold on well enough. It needs
only that I boil the water and pour instead
of relying on automatic bells and whistles,
preprogramming, and so forth.

                       You recall
those TV commercials in the seventies
where Joe DiMaggio sold MR. COFFEE®
saying that the electric heating gizmo
brought water not to a boil, but the perfect temperature
for coffee, which was 180 degrees or something?
Grandma's pot, with not even an ON/OFF switch,
makes better coffee! One English guest compared
this "system" to the use of a teaspoon
with which Brits stir not just to mix the milk
or lemon, but to cool their tea. Likewise,
when I pour boiling water in the top,
while the liquid's waiting in the upper reservoir,
the metal pot cools it, so by the time
it drips down past the tiny holes and through
the coffee, it's the perfect temperature!

Of course I don't wake to a just-made pot
of coffee, but the point's to wake up, no?
Doing instead of having something done
helps in this morning process. Plus, the grounds
are fresh-scooped—fresh-ground when I want—not out

all night, getting stale. And Grandma's pot
will never go on the blink.

                           So you're invited
for a cup of coffee, the best you'll ever have,
and for a verse of poetry, or Shakespeare.
I have not only a COMPLETE WORKS here,
I'm pretty sure I have a spare somewhere
to take down and dust off. Or we can share.

Sylvius

He and his love were fictional, of course.
And anyhow by now I'm sure they're dead!—
And yet, in the performance, real: The source
Of true love never can run just the head
Even if prison'd in the imagination.
An audience might gape if not guffaw
At his delight in willing degradation.
Yet his will seems to fill mine own with awe,
Inspiring with the depth of his prostration
If not his love for—Phoebe, was her name?—
And how, enrapt, he found some words to say
Unchecked by unsurpassed exasperation.
Were I to love I might well act the same.
Meanwhile I have two tickets to the play. . . .

(Sylvius and Phoebe are characters in
Shakespeare's *As You Like It*)

Othello

What a pause he took
and still not long enough.

What a horrible word is *husband*
etymologically;
the verb implies such unbecoming things
and challenges the man to be a "man"
when a human not a monster
is what's called for.

What general, what warrior,
might not fear turning into a, what, a wimp
when faced with lies in a situation
fooling himself his act's a sign of strength?

And where's the man that doesn't care
what others think, that can't be shamed,
and cannot be convinced of a cause
that introspection hasn't tested?

Only the poet, the moral arbiter,
I think. And that is why poetry

must still be taught in schools, not simply
reading, but thinking, feeling, scratching,
honing, coming up with your own
right thoughts and best words in best
orders, able to overthrow

millennia of crap when it
is common sense to do so,

even if—especially if—
no one's thought before of what
the poet or the thinker dares
to think, or even—especially—admit.

If Othello were a poet, not
merely a warrior, Desdemona
would still be alive today.
If you are, then the planet has
a chance.

Every soldier—every husband, too—
even the one—especially the one—
who'll tend The Button on Judgment Day—
should know Othello,
should dabble in poetry
so as not to keep on making such mistakes.

Bachelor Actor

He was as cumulus clouds in a bright blue sky—
you could never reach him, no less touch him, but
he'd float there, Casper-friendly, contented—containing,
until the sun dipped low as the day wore on
and the same clouds started turning indigo
then into the black of night, ominous,
where they'd been—that is, he'd been—luminous
but moments before. Then while the rest of us gathered
our things and talked about dinner plans, he'd
vanish like a puff in the air, unnoticed,
gone.

He never dined or went out for a beer
with us. The topics never even came up,
because whatever cloud hung over him
each evening was replaced each morning as
cumulus clouds in a background of balmy blue.
He was so fun, in fact, no one recalled,
during the seven bright hours, how dark
he'd suddenly become, the previous day's eighth.
So no one thought to ask him, say at lunch,
hey, whatcha doin' tonight? We were, by each
day's sudden vanishing trick, daily
surprised.

The actresses wondered if he was still single,
and if so, why. Some of the actors
suspected he might not have been into
ladies. I noted—silently, of course—
he didn't seem to be much into them,
either. As the director, I am grateful

that he was smart as the head of any class,
trim as a matinée idol, lithe
as a serpent, and playing Iago
to perfection.

Simon Stimson

Gossip is the mighty sorcerer who
without so much as an abracadabra
takes the diamond of your soul
and makes it—poof—disappear
so that you die alone, unsung,
while all the rest of the best of you—
your childhood promise, adolescent ardor,
the discipline, drive, resilience
of your young adult years—gets
eaten, as the magician swallows
desultory goldfish, or pins on strings,
or razor blades, or knives, or as
the dervish downs hot, dazzling fire.
Gossip, however, does not
spit out the fire but digests it,
never to shit it out, oh no,
but to grow fat on it forevermore.
And there you are, inside his gut,
churned by the acid of the future until
if you are lucky, after you are dead,

Gossip, again by magic, wakes you up.

And Your Name, like a half-hatched memory,
and your quickless heart, walk Your Town again,
till the Nasty Thing gets said again. And if
you've been given your ears back too (although
you don't really need to hear the words, you've heard—
overheard—them all before, and know
the face, the snicker, and the shh) you wish
you were back home, up on the hill,
even though there's a mob of pewling umbrellas

blocking the way. But should you go back now
no one will see you. They're all thinking of
the Other, a recent arrival in the yard—
it's only one or two who'd straggled by
and seen your name and called you up,
for a moment only. So you do go back,

grateful this time that Gossip is a sorcerer
and can make things like them and you poof disappear,
and you let your mound get overgrown
and let the name fade from your stone,
as all the forget-me-nots turn into
moss, dirt, roots, mulch, brown crinkling
remains of leaves, and the gnarly welters of
scentless, stinking,
noiseless, noisome
overripe
oblivion.

       (Simon Stimson, the musician/misanthrope in *Our Town*)

One of Ours

Anne made Helen one of ours
    and famous to this day,
but it's she the title of the play
by William Gibson (which made stars
of Anne Bancroft and Patty Duke)
refers to—Annie Sullivan,
as grand a soul, though half the name,
    for the miracle she worked.

Had someone said to me *You can!*
    when I was Keller's age
(and not just as a passing joke)
    I might have been the same
and you'd be seeing *me* onstage,
    rapt in craft or fame.

You laugh, and yet might I suggest
that *you* can triumph if you choose
    to go, and do your best?

What have you, after all, to lose,
    but me and tutelage?—
And we were only here to use.

So go now, north, south, east or west.

    Besides, I need the rest.

Boo Radley's House

You wouldn't recognize "our house" (the one
we told the kids in the cast was Boo Rad-
ley's, *you* know, with the junk in front?). They've done
it up as a Painted Lady, trimly clad
in beige, light blue and mauve. (The junk is gone.)

Since we're presenting *Our Town* this year, we
had wedding and choir scenes, the funeral,
and two younger siblings to cast. There's three
new children, who are pretty good, but all
the *Mockingbird* kids are cast, happily.

Our Dills and Jems stand higher by half a head
this season, and advance a little slower;
nor do they pounce and squirm but sit instead.
Their jokes sound about half an octave lower
and tend to turn each others' faces red.

Our Scouts tote pocket books and make less noise.
Remember how Tracey (one Scout) would race
to the swinging tire at break, and beat the boys?
Now, neither one would dream of giving chase
but bead their brows and smile with pointed poise.

And all six appear quite at home onstage,
too serious to ask *Who killed the mock-
ingbird?!* as they did last year. Past the age
of giggling and guffawing now, they *talk!*—
in shades of mostly mauve, light blue and beige.

(Scout, Jem and Dill, the three major child roles in the stage
version of *To Kill a Mockingbird*, are often double-cast
when productions involve school-day matinées)

The Loud One

I went to visit a high school class
performing musical theater, Les Miz,
and singled out an unsung sophomore
singing her heart out as if destitute.
She had a beauty mark or rash
high on her right cheek, which resembled, in the shadows
of those chorusing left and right of her,
a black eye, which made her look like Cosette.
And how she sang her heart out. And then beamed
when I talked about singing your heart out
and the French revolution of 1830,
and classes, and poverty, and hope and despair,
and the things that the story was about.

Later the instructor told me it was great
that I mentioned her, she never gets mentioned,
and always sings from the pit of her heart
and I said that I think it's been long enough
that the loud ones have played all the roles, or leads,
which isn't what the modern drama needs.

He asked how so, I told him how one time
one loud one even convinced the rest
of the world that his was the only role
for awhile, so that everyone else would only
be arrivistes at best. The acting
teacher had a degree, of course, and asked
What, you mean someone in Greece, and I
said, even before that, there was a Man
who rewrote the script so that he'd be the hero
and the play the Original Playwright wrote

has been all but lost with all the improvisation,
interpolation, and rewriting of
the loud one known as Man. At least
Nick Bottom, who wanted to play all the roles,
was guileless, filled with bonhomie,
indisputably fictional,
and bowed when summoned to perform
to the Duke and his bride, who'd been queen of the
        Amazons.
—Mann, not Thomas? Austrian? German?
How come I never heard of him?
—You probably know him in the allegory,
as Adam. —Which means, what, The Loud One?
—Well no but yes. —Hm. No but yes? —
The word Adam meaning, in whatever language, Man.

Misanthrope

Would you incur the insight of the skeptic
Who suffers the society of fools
As rudely as the stricken epileptic
Who throbs and howls and cannot follow rules?
Of course not. Therefore keep me out of sight,
Particularly when you know I'm right.

Tip from the Taxi Driver

"What Am I Doing Here?" —"What Are *We*?" Call it
the secret of the Cosmos—call me daft—
but once, when I was opening my wallet

about to tip a taxi driver, all at
once, he—he answered, then winked. I—I *laughed*.
What was I doing there? What was he? Call it

what you want, but to hear the fellow tell it
you too would know: *He knew!* . . . A good week aft-
erwards, when I was opening my wallet

to tip another taxi driver, well, it
came to me in a flash (I'm not that swift,
see). I was here, and he was there, and—call it

a voice or a beatitude, but will it
matter? . . . So the next time you get a lift
in a cab, when you're opening your wallet,

pay heed to what your cabbie says. Then mull it
over. Ask him to repeat. Once you've left,
What We Are Doing Here—you won't recall it!
And do not rush when opening your wallet.

(after Leonard Melfi's "Teaser's Taxi")

The Wit

The wit knows he is not a winner.
    Not, at least, politically.
Nor the so-persuasive sinner
    he might like to be.

But he lobs a silky spark
    to brighten where we couldn't see
only to delight the dark
    temporarily.

frostbite #9: A Penny Balanced

I thought about that penny on the ground
and flipping it over or not for the next soul to find
and then thought that if it were suspended on a wire
held taut, there's no way it could stay there, it would have
to fall to one side or the other, just as

a play becomes a comedy or tragedy;
and that the planet the penny was sitting on
is held in space taut as that stretched-out wire,
so that the penny was going to have to flip
some time or other; and that we're only in

act two or three of a four or five act play,
which means there's time for the whole thing to switch
from comedy to tragedy, as when Mercutio kills
Tybalt, accidentally, under Romeo's arm,

or tragedy to comedy, as in so many tales
where the situation, what with all the poverty
and wartime strife, must be sufficiently
"tragic to be comic," as they say.

And so whether I flipped it or not would depend on the
          course
I thought the penny was on, the planet, that is,
and what act we were in, were there time for a switch

to steer us to a happy ending, or
were we on our way inexorably to the unspeakable.
I hovered awhile, then decided. Do you remember?

Δ

Oh sure, that penny was only a metaphor,
but metaphor is myth, untrue

but more true, and deserving of consideration.
And now that you've seen a penny first, it's your turn.

And not to flip, or even not to think,

would be a choice as well. O the suspense.

You've been asked to think about it, and here's the penny.

Our road is one; the divergence, in your hands.

Act Three

To a Dancer, Age Plenty-Nine

Your foot moved to the left, mine to the right,
And everything was altered. On that day,
We danced, and the world was filled with light.

You were already what I saw I might
Become. A Dancer. You would show the way,
Your foot slid to the left, mine to the right—

My right, your left. No fledgling's taken flight
More born than I. There was nothing to say.
We danced, and the world was bathed in light.

When did you know? Was it a normal sight,
A novice turning to a protégée?
Your foot flexed to the left, mine to the right,

Reflecting, as in glass: Whatever slight
Adjustment, do-si-do, or relevé
You danced, I danced, and danced on, soaked in light.

And there are great moves left! It's not yet night!
For you are here, and that's the brightest ray,
Your left toe tapping left, my right toe, right:
We're dancing, and the world is full of light.

(Honoring the legacy of Bella Malinka)

Denizen

Twenty-two on Broadway,
  Then a touring show.
Not a lot since then, but jobs
  Are hard to land, we know.

Used to be the friendliest
  Of faces in the hall;
Now his eyes float by downcast
  Or glued against the wall.

Now his hair is falling out
  And what is left is gray.
Now there aren't so many calls
  To hoof it on Broadway.

Law & Order once or twice
  But once he had to speak,
Forgot his line. They've not called since.
  He watches every week.

But he was more a dancer
  Than a speaker or a star.
Now he is a denizen
  Like so many of us are.

In the Dimness

I met a man who said he'd been looking most of his life
      only to find
that it was never there, the thing that he was looking for,
and looked back now and regretted just about everything,
one way or the other. At least, that's what he said.
He'd made his million, maybe two, said he had a man for
      counting,
but what did he have to show for it, he asked. He liked my
      songs,
he said, stuck a sawbuck in the snifter, and bought the
      room a round.
He didn't partake anymore, himself, he said. It was an off
      night,
a small crowd, off-season, but they all swayed to my music
and stayed long. When he went to the loo, that's what he
      called the john,
everybody said What a nice man. They called him by his
      first name.
My name was on the placard out front, but no one ever said
      it,
they just requested music. He came back and told them all
that they had to stuff the snifter, too, and they did. On my
      breaks
I listened at his table with the others. And I told him
that I thought he had nothing to regret, that that was a dim
      view
of everything, and all he'd done and not done, tried and
      didn't,
that it was just the way, in the general scheme of things,
for us all to be here tonight, together, with this music,
      wasn't it magical,

and everyone agreed with me, and bucked him on the
    back,
and clapped for me and slapped their extra bills and filled
    my snifter.
I told him money's money, but it's more—a metaphor.
For what? Can't say, I said, then told him *he'd* found, and
    gave, and got,
after hours, tonight, what *I'd* spent most of my life looking
    for.
Then in the dimness I saw him smile a second or so, I
    thought.

Defiance

You stumble, through your character, at the end
of a long lapse and grumble in defiance.
What have you now but Nothing? Every friend
has passed on; neighbors pause but never lend
an ear; your faith, its blind and blithe reliance
on formulas, is futile. Don't pretend
there's more than loitering and cracking wise
with howls of *Heck*s and *Drat*s, *Consarn*s and *Fie*s.

But do the dance you know can make it rain
to drown the imprecations of the wife
offstage, as evanescent now as life:
Brandish bold saws again to thrive again:
Inveigh the heavens: Curse us, every one:
Go on!—that I might see how it is done.

(after H. M. Koutoukas, 1937-2010)

And Charlie Chaplin is no more

And Charlie Chaplin is no more.
　　The Tramp's long laid to rest.
And nothing is that was before
　　his sun set in the west.

He made us laugh. He made the poor,
　　with every new release,
what audiences rooted for.
　　And now he rests in peace

and silent, in the video store,
　　collected in a box
beyond the *Action!* and the *Gore*
　　on the shelf that never talks.

The speechless hobo, though inept,
　　was feisty in his fight.
But no one takes him home, except
　　the very erudite.

Still fewer know the silent heart
　　nor wail for waifs or masses;
those predisposed to take his part
　　dozed at their film classes.

The city's like a ghetto now
　　walled in by a giant screen
that only shows what dons allow
　　from lairs unknown, unseen.

Elders, who once climbed the height
　　and saw the West, have said

that the endless road's now endless night.
 And Charlie Chaplin's dead.

But I, refusing to forget
 or to believe, protest
by buying an entire boxed set
 of the tramp who headed west.

And though I know his hopeful sun
 shone only in black-and-white
I flip them through and pick out one
 as silent as tonight

about the clown who had no name
 and now, in silence, load—
to see the sun, in the final frame,
 set on an open road.

Miss Lee

She had the cognac voice, the brandy breast,
the corrugated heart, as iron as
the mullion giving panes the strength to hold.
A bout of *Fever* gave her discernible flaws,
a nick in the ribbing, a bubble in the glass.

But how she fought. How many comebacks can
you count to? The one Goodman in her life
died young, but she sang on, ran off, sang on,
and disappeared, then crooned and wrote again.
Now the iron, the glass, the ribs, the bubbles, are gone.

I have but one of her, in vinyl, scratched,
and set it spinning on the turntable,
sitting by my window with a shot
of something, wondering *Is that all there is?*—
then pour another, wishing it were not.

(Peggy Lee, 1920 - 2002)

Mister Gray

Mister Gray, Mister Gray,
why'd you have to go that way?
I saw you play in *Our Town* and
your speeches helped me understand,
but didn't you believe in what
you said? Oh, Mister Gray, you cut
me to the quick. Were you depressed?
Over-needy of a rest?
But you had children; I do not.
In fact, I haven't got a lot.
You also had a loving wife.
How could you go take your life?
And oh, what's done can't be undone.
If that's the example set by one
as successful and talented as you,
what's someone like me supposed to do?

(Spalding Gray, actor, author, 1941-2004)

AmeriCulture Festival 2001

On with the show, you've heard. And we go on
with practice and with putting on a play
in honor of all that's so soon, too soon, gone—

the next performance, as the summer season—
and cherish one another, as we say
On with the show. You've heard how we go on

no matter what. It's difficult at dawn,
actors are not morning people, but they,
in honor of what's so soon, too soon, gone,

put out 200 percent, like no one
else, every day. Or almost every day.
On with the sh—Ah, you've heard. Well, we went on

the 13th, but the 12th, sat on the lawn,
held hands, prayed—even those who did not pray—
in honor of who were so soon, too soon, gone

that bright September in 2001
that stopped the show, once. But we've found our way.
On with the show, we say, now, and go on
in honor of all that's so soon, too soon, gone.

1985

The phone rang weekly in that early age
of ringing, wringing out ammonia tears,
when the plague was new. Actors of too few years
and roles were lost, too many ghosts of stage
and film too quickly made. Now, calls from lover,
spouse or sibling are rarer, but not over.

Were you to phone today and tell me that
you'd found my number starred beside my name
in his black book, and thought that you should take
the time to dial me up and tell me what
he'd thought of me, that I was not the same
as others he'd known, I'd ask *When's the wake?*
and tell you to be glad that you're alive.

I might not have, in 1985.

The Dark Act

The remembered were remembered in the rain,
under the black umbrellas of *Our Town,*
and the forgotten were forgotten again,

while Thornton Wilder lives on. In Camden,
Walt Whitman grew old, and he kept on hon-
ing, that he be remembered in the rain.

In Arles, where Vincent might have gone insane,
crows beckoned, wheat fields glowed an eerie brown
and the forgotten were forgotten again.

Salinger's self-exile: our loss, his gain;
but he'd achieved already such renown
the he would be remembered in the rain.

As for Emily in Amherst: it is plain
whom Thornton named Emily for in his town
so she would not be forgotten again.

Delay it as you embrace it! Need I explain,
we both live in a dark act of our own
where the remembered are remembered in the rain,
and the forgotten are forgotten again and again?

American Sequel

A play reverts to nothing when it's done,
nothing save the potential to fulfill
what it was asking. But we never do,
it seems, not that we can't or never will,
but have been trained to play incessantly
with love and hope the clamor of Act One
and are so proud of what we have begun
and so enjoy the promise of Act Two
we never see the point in playing Three.

Lincoln Center

Your first time there, if it is day, you might
find the marble walls and pavings too sleek,
clean, cold and gray for life; the panels packed
as snug as drawers at a morgue. Three slabs stand still,
remote and firm as guards at a museum;
their aspects interest only for their façades.
Aliens probably placed the buildings there
as monuments to mark their mausoleum.

But in the evening, edges blur. The light
shoots out the windows as if it would speak
and draws you in. The crystal fountain's spell
summons the dead to dance or sing or act
and suddenly they've turned to demigods
come back to us with movement everywhere.

Leonard Bernstein:
Young People's Concert

1.

All

We had to do
No matter what
No matter who

Was sit
In gently arced
Rows
In his direction

And listen.

And he
Gave us music:

When the music stopped,
Himself;

And loved us
No matter who
No matter what.

All

2.

His baton
His arms
His eyes

His voice
Transmuted into the orchestra's
Sensations
Which enveloped us
Through ears
To toes
In his wide embrace
Even as his back was to us.

Today I understand, that's why he bounced
Why he had to bounce
Tiptoe and back down
When he extended his stick:

He had a world, in one direction, to create;
Another world, in the other, to reach;

So his passion turned rapture
And he leaped over time
(Transforming it to tempo) and
Space, and the distance
Between became naught;
His baton, a wand.

3.

No, this is not my poetic imagination
Or invention working. For, decades later,
At a Dramatists Guild 25th-anniversary symposium
On the creation of *West Side Story*,
After he walked down the aisle right past me
On his way to the stage with the others,
And I was too slow to grasp that the four were entering
Through the center aisle,
Too slow to grasp him when he passed by,

I saw how he, arriving on the stage,
Embraced the other three
Creators—
Literally, I mean, with his arms,
His all—

And then, turning to us,
Through the magic of his presence, not just music,
Talking to us when the music stopped, he
Reached out and
Loved us again no matter
Who or
What or
How—

All.

Beethoven's Fifth

The repetition, then the variation,
separated us from the animals,
he said. Len Bernstein. That was composition.

Young People's Concert. TV. Repetition,
when chosen, was how we knew we had souls.
The repetition, then the variation,

dadada dum... as if in invitation,
and then DADADA *DUM!* How one phrase calls—
as for an answer: that was composition.

He said it again. The swelling excitation
swelled into fervor, sounding off the walls,
in repetition and more variation,

as beads fell from his hair, though that rendition
was stop and go, 'cause Bernstein had the balls
to stop the orchestra, explaining composition

to all of us. His patient explanation,
his kind way—I was five and felt His thrills.
The repetition, then the variation,
he said, was what made us—and composition!

The Silver Slipper

Even Amanda Wingfield worshiped—or,
if *worship* jars you, let us say *adore*—
a crescent moon, like the one now taking aim
from its canvas of dappled, transient indigo.
On a flag, of course, it cannot glow the same
as in an evening's sentimental sky:
But I don't fear its subjects! Yes, I know
Amanda was but a role in a play
and fictional, but so are you and I,
my fearsome, fearing friend, in a way,
and born to be forgotten, one day.

> (In Tennessee Williams's *The Glass Menagerie*, Amanda
> Wingfield has her daughter Laura make a wish on the
> "little silver slipper of a moon" at the end of Act I)

Only I

Only I
Saw the fly
Flitter by
The actor's eye

Saw him flick it with a finger
Saw the thing fly back and linger
Make him blink and make him twitch
Most would think he had an itch

He never dropped a line or cue
For that is not what actors do
But focused on the space between
On the objective and the scene

When the fly leapt to my lap
I slew it with a sudden slap
The actor heard but was not riled
Just looked my way and smiled

The Rest

The rest is silence, Hamlet said.
But some, while sleeping, snore;
some dream: and as for being dead
(to extend the metaphor)
some are written down, and even read.

World

Imagine if you can a jet black backdrop. Imagine if you can
a London day, in front of which players emote and hop
according to the dictates of a play. When Shakespeare
said that All the world's a stage, absent the script and
actors you'd have been transported to a literary age
from late morning till two or three, say, in

the afternoon, lit, bustling. In the modern world, though,
take the play away, and you'd be in a great dark empty
hall, now awed by the darkness and emptiness. You
oohed and ahed for hours so delightfully that now in
their remembrance, and the hall's unbearable
bleakness, or just to see if someone else is sitting in the
stalls,

you start imagining another drama, and the light spills from
the floorboards to the audience, and once again you're
calm, half-certain someone's watching it with you.

You go on like this till you realize that you've become a
hack, just to survive and palliate the absence of the
light. It's been enough, but suddenly—surprise, it is no
more. You'd rather be alive for real and feel the
pounding of your heart and others', and for the first
time you start thinking about forever—and rewrite,

haunted by jet-black, trying to assuage the backdrop as you
stare at the egg-white blankness of one leaf, just before
the page absorbs the bright new world you'll dream
tonight.

Supplemental Notes

5 [The Beauty of Actors] Last two lines: One origin myth of Aphrodite, goddess of beauty and love, is that she emerged out of the sea foam off the island of Cyprus.

12-13 [Educational Drama] Proper names mentioned are roles in *Romeo and Juliet*. Stanza 5, p. 13: Some college drama programs participate in the American College Theater Festival where colleagues are invited to attend their productions and nominate students for awards. Regional winners attend the national festival at the Kennedy Center in Washington, DC. These nominators also give a critique, called a "response," to cast and crew, and so are called "respondents."

22-23 [A Broadway Show] Stanza 2: Laurette Taylor created the role of Amanda Wingfield in *The Glass Menagerie*, by Tennessee Williams. Her variations on the dialogue were recorded for future productions in the acting edition, which is now out of print. Stanza 6, p. 23: The Nederlander Organization sold the Mark Hellinger Theater on West 51st Street to the Times Square Church in 1991.

45 ["The Producers"] When the musical version of Mel Brooks's movie opened on Broadway, some critics took exception to his light treatment of such a horrible thing as the Holocaust.

55 [Play] Stanzas 3-4: George Reeves and Dean Cain played Superman on TV; Christopher Reeve, on film. Festus, Miss Kitty and Matt Dillon were characters, and James Arness and Amanda Blake were actors, in the CBS western *Gunsmoke*, TV's longest running prime-time drama until NBC's *Law and Order*.

57 [On Staging . . .] and 58 [Antigone] Haemon, Ismene, Eurydice and Creon are characters in the Greek tragedy *Antigone,* wherein no one can convince the heroine not to do the right thing, even though it's against the law. Most are dead by play's end.

59 [Fate] Stanza 3: "Upstart crow": a critic's epithet for William Shakespeare when he was an up-and-comer. "Queen": One rumor still circulates that Elizabeth I wrote the plays attributed to him. Stanza 4: *dramatis personae:* cast of characters.

60 [Yesterday's Man] *sous-sol:* French. Literally "underground," or basement.

61 [Hellsgate] Morality plays often exhibited a grotesque Head of Hellsgate, mouth agape, as a visual reminder of where a sinner would be headed if he did not change his ways. Stanza 1: *Mummers* were itinerant performers.

66-69 [Othello, Bachelor Actor] Quick plot summary of the Shakespeare tragedy: Jealousy, the "green-eyed *monster,*" (stanza 2, p. 66) drives Othello, the warrior-husband, to slay his faithful wife Desdemona. He is convinced, erroneously, that she has sinned against him. Iago (p. 69) is the villain who does the convincing.

68 [see also above note] Stanza 1: *Casper the Friendly Ghost* was a popular cartoon and comic book.

70 [Simon Stimson] Act III of *Our Town* takes place in the graveyard on the hill, whose "residents," including Stimson, kibitz during a funeral in the rain.

72 [One of Ours] William Gibson's *The Miracle Worker* re-

106

lates the story of blind-and-deaf Helen Keller and her teacher Annie Sullivan. Patty Duke and Anne Bancroft created the roles on Broadway and won Oscars for their film reprises.

73 [Boo Radley's House] Radley is a fearsome, mysterious character in Harper Lee's *To Kill a Mockingbird*, rarely stepping foot outside his home—until the children need him.

74 [The Loud One] Stanza 1: Cosette is the rags-to-riches (orphan-to-aristocrat) role in Victor Hugo's novel *Les Misérables*, the stage musical of which is known colloquially as Les Miz. Stanza 3, p. 75: Nick Bottom is an enthusiastic amateur actor in Shakespeare's *A Midsummer Night's Dream*.

76 [The Misanthrope] Though the title role in a play by Molière, The Misanthrope, like The Cynic, has appeared as a supporting role-type in drama since ancient times.

79 [frostbite #9: A Penny Balanced] The title refers to Robert Frost's famous poem "The Road Not Taken," where "Two roads diverged in a yellow wood...." Stanzas 1-4: Many have noted that *Romeo and Juliet* seems to be a comedy until the slaying of Tybalt midway through.

88 *[And Charlie Chaplin is no more]* Stanza 1: The Tramp was Charlie Chaplin's hapless persona in many films, mostly silent ones.

90 [Miss Lee] Peggy Lee often sang with jazz great Benny Goodman. "Fever" and "Is That All There Is?" are two of her hit songs (though not with Goodman).

92 The AmeriCulture Festival, in Fitchburg, Mass., fea-

tured productions of plays and other art-related events.

94 [The Dark Act] Stanzas 1-2, 6: See note for p. 70, above. Thornton Wilder named his *Our Town* heroine for Emily Dickinson, who lived in Amherst, Mass. Poet Walt Whitman lived his last years in Camden, NJ. Stanza 3: Vincent Van Gogh lived and painted in Arles, France, among other places; *Crows in a Wheatfield* was putatively his last painting. Stanza 4: J. D. Salinger, author of *Catcher in the Rye*, withdrew from the public eye to a private life in Cornish, New Hampshire.

97 [Leonard Bernstein] and 100 [Beethoven's Fifth] Bernstein was a conductor, composer and social activist. His Young People's Concerts were televised on PBS in the 'fifties and 'sixties and are available on DVD. I highly recommend them.

102 *[Only I]* My friend Erin Lee Kelly sat in the front row at *The Gin Game* on Broadway and told me of this particular fly. The actor was James Earl Jones. Stanza 4 is my invention.

103 [The Rest] The quote is Hamlet's last four words before dying, in Act V.

104 [World] Stanza 1: "All the world's a stage" begins Jaques's famous speech in *As You Like It*, Act II scene 7.

About the Author

With his first collection of poetry, *Manhattan Plaza*,
James B. Nicola follows poets Elizabeth Bishop, Frank
O'Hara and Stanley Kunitz and humorist Robert Benchley
as a New York author hailing from Worcester, Massachu-
setts. James has been widely published in periodicals in-
cluding *Tar River*, *Lyric*, *Nimrod*, *Blue Unicorn* and the
Southwest, *Atlanta*, *Lullwater*, and *Texas Reviews*, state-
side, and overseas in *The Istanbul Review*, *Poetry Salzburg*,
The Recusant, *Antiphon*, *Sand*, and *Snakeskin*. He also won
the Dana Literary Award, a People's Choice award (from
Storyteller) and a *Willow Review* award; was nominated
twice for a Pushcart Prize and once for a Rhysling Award;
and was featured poet at *New Formalist*. A graduate of Yale
and a stage director by profession, his nonfiction book
Playing the Audience won a *Choice* award. Also a com-
poser, lyricist, and playwright, his children's musical
Chimes: A Christmas Vaudeville premiered in Fairbanks,
Alaska, where Santa Claus was rumored to be in attend-
ance on opening night.

About the Artist

Eve Sonneman is an internationally known photographer
and painter. Her books include *REAL TIME, Roses are Red*
with Klaus Kertess, *America's Cottage Gardens*, *Where
Birds Live* (introduction by Adam Gopnik), and *How to
Touch What* with Lawrence Weiner. To find out more, go to
www.evesonneman.com.

Reaction to Manhattan Plaza :

[In] James B. Nicola's book *Manhattan Plaza,* New York [City's] bursting with life as it constantly reinvents itself.... Nicola's fertile world [is]... dramatic, exciting, comfortable, uneasy and intriguing. But Nicola does not neglect the necessity to work on our inner selves.... Nicola never lacks his own center and doesn't mutate into those around him, with nature ever-present to help despite buildings so high they might make us feel insignificant and crowds so large that they threaten to force us into anonymity.... The poet himself is mentally and emotionally on fire, as each image merges into the next amidst his reflections.... This is a book that extroverts and poets will immediately understand... from a fresh new voice who loves people and thrives on living among them. While reading this book I wanted to jump on a plane and visit New York City again....

—Christina Zawadiwsky, *FutureCycle*

The subject of Nicola's debut collection is not a far off place in the imagination, but one grounded solidly in the real world with real inhabitants. The concrete here is literal, the view, populated with a kind of human spirit that for all its Americanism, also exhibits traits so universal, it often aches.... [R]eader alongside speaker, two "like-minded observers," together [bear] witness to the inner workings of Manhattan. We travel like blood through veins of a body that remains (at times sadly) unaware of our presence... Through this gazing, frequently voyeuristic and exploitive, at other moments painfully tender, but always with a sense of obligatory honesty, the reader too has no choice but to be forever transformed.... [Always] the journey is more important than the destination, which is the chance to restore meaning to a city where "everything is strange and new.".... At the conclusion of the collection, I was left homesick for a place I have never had the pleasure of calling home.

—April Salzano, *blackandwhitegetsread.blogspot.com*

Nicola adopts the mantle of facilitator, guide, and keen observer.... [The] introductory flourish quickly establishes Nicola's voice and humor as both a relatable and insightful guide.... Streets and stanzas ... make for vivid encounters and oblique rumination.... The book's final pages are filled with hospitality, vulnerability, and reflection, mingling a confessional style with surveys of places and people. Nicola's integrative style allows him to render abstractions – of history, of the city–personal. Perhaps one of Nicola's greatest accomplishments in adopting this style is his investigation of the lingering wounds wrought by the September 11th terrorist attacks on the nation, the city, and himself.

—Shawn Bodden, *Green Hills Literary Lantern*

James B. Nicola's *Manhattan Plaza*... is structured with the thoughtfulness of an architect's blueprint or a tour guide's Baedeker.... It reads as colloquially and on as tight a stage as Frank O'Hara's "The Day Lady Died".... But it also travels out as all Manhattan dwellers do onto the broader stage, as grand as Walt Whitman's "Crossing Brooklyn Ferry".... Throughout..., Nicola employs a versatility of rhyming verse; free, couplet, quatrain.... Nicola's laser not only illuminates the nitty-gritty, but it also echoes the journey of T. S. Eliot's "Little Gidding:" ... "to arrive where we started/And know the place for the first time." *Manhattan Plaza* reads like a biography or memoir.... [A]fter all our wanderings and wonderings: "We have become New York."

—Burnham Holmes, *Vermont Literary Review*

Made in the USA
Middletown, DE
19 May 2016